In memory of Etheridge Knight, Phyllis Tickle, and Memphis in 1978.
—A.F.D.

To my parents, for their boundless love and support.
—X.G.

STERLING CHILDREN'S BOOKS
New York

An Imprint of Sterling Publishing Co., Inc.
1166 Avenue of the Americas
New York, NY 10036

STERLING CHILDREN'S BOOKS and the distinctive Sterling Children's Books logo are registered trademarks of Sterling Publishing Co., Inc.

Text © 2019 Alice Faye Duncan
Illustrations © 2019 Xia Gordon
The poems of Gwendolyn Brooks are reprinted with consent of Brooks Permissions.

ISBN 978-1-4549-3088-4

Distributed in Canada by Sterling Publishing Co., Inc.
c/o Canadian Manda Group, 664 Annette Street
Toronto, Ontario M6S 2C8, Canada
Distributed in the United Kingdom by GMC Distribution Services
Castle Place, 166 High Street, Lewes, East Sussex BN7 1XU, England
Distributed in Australia by NewSouth Books
45 Beach Street, Coogee, NSW 2034, Australia

For information about custom editions, special sales, and premium and corporate purchases, please contact Sterling Special Sales at 800-805-5489 or specialsales@sterlingpublishing.com.

Manufactured in China

Lot #:
2 4 6 8 10 9 7 5 3 1
10/18

sterlingpublishing.com

Jacket and interior design by Irene Vandervoort

The time
cracks into furious flower. Lifts its face
all unashamed.

—*Gwendolyn Brooks*

A Song for
GWENDOLYN
BROOKS

ALICE FAYE DUNCAN

ILLUSTRATED BY
XIA GORDON

STERLING CHILDREN'S BOOKS
New York

I
SING a song for Gwendolyn Brooks.
Sing it loud—a Chicago blues.

Skip to the beat of elevated trains.
They grumble, rumble, and roll real fast.

The year is 1925.
Gwendolyn Brooks is eight years old.

Gray bursts of smoke hide the yellow sun.
Can flowers grow without sunlight?

Gwendolyn leans on the front yard gate.
Gwendolyn is unsure.

II
SING a song for Gwendolyn Brooks.
She greets each day in her velvet glory.

Her head is filled with snappy rhymes.
She writes her poems in dime store
   journals.

Gwendolyn stands outside the fray.
Her classmates cuss.
They swish and sass.

THE BUSY CLOCK

Clock, clock tell the time,
Tell the time to me.
Magic, patient instrument,
That is never free.

Tick, tock, busy clock!
You've no time to play.
Bustling men and women
Need you all the day.

—1928

They joke and jive.
They laugh real loud.

They boast and bully.
They "signify."

Girls jump rope on cracked sidewalks.
Boys play baseball in the streets.

Poets own a watchful eye.
Gwendolyn stands alone.

III
SING a song for Gwendolyn Brooks.

Her father is a janitor.
He buys the food and pays the rent.

"Mothering" is her mama's job.
She cooks the food and scrubs the clothes.

Baby Brother is Gwen's best friend.
They play checkers on rainy days.

When the sky is blue,
Gwendolyn sits with her tattered notebooks.

From the top step of her backyard porch,
She watches and listens to the South Side neighbors.

Women talk about men.
Men talk about sports.
Children call Gwen—"ol' stuck-up heifer!"

IV
SING a song for Gwendolyn Brooks.
Her mother believes.
Her father believes.

But sometimes—Gwendolyn doubts her radiance,
When jarring, crashing, discordant words,
Splotch and splatter her notebook paper.

And when RIGHT words don't crystallize,
Gwendolyn grabs her mother's garden trowel.

She digs beneath the snowball bush,
And buries her poems in a backyard grave.

V
SING a song for Gwendolyn Brooks.
She is a student at Forestville School.

Miss Schoolteacher sends a letter home.
It reads, "Gwendolyn is a cheat. She plagiarized."

Gwendolyn is a cheat?

This is not so.
Mama grabs her hat, black purse, and gloves.
She marches Gwendolyn to the school.
Mrs. Brooks defends her precocious child.

She says, "Miss Schoolteacher! I must protest.
Gwendolyn does not need to cheat.
She writes and speaks with the finest ease.
Test her now and we will see."

Gwendolyn considers the insulting charge.
She writes a poem in proud, prim letters.

FORGIVE AND FORGET

If others neglect you,
Forget; do not sigh,
For, after all, they'll select you
In times by and by.
If their taunts cut and hurt you,
They are sure to regret.
And if in time, they desert you,
Forgive and forget.

—1928

Miss Schoolteacher must drop her charge.
Gwen steps high on her walk home.

Gwen smiles brightly.
Gwen BELIEVES.

And as the sun breaks through gray clouds of smoke,
Sunlight shines on Gwendolyn's face.

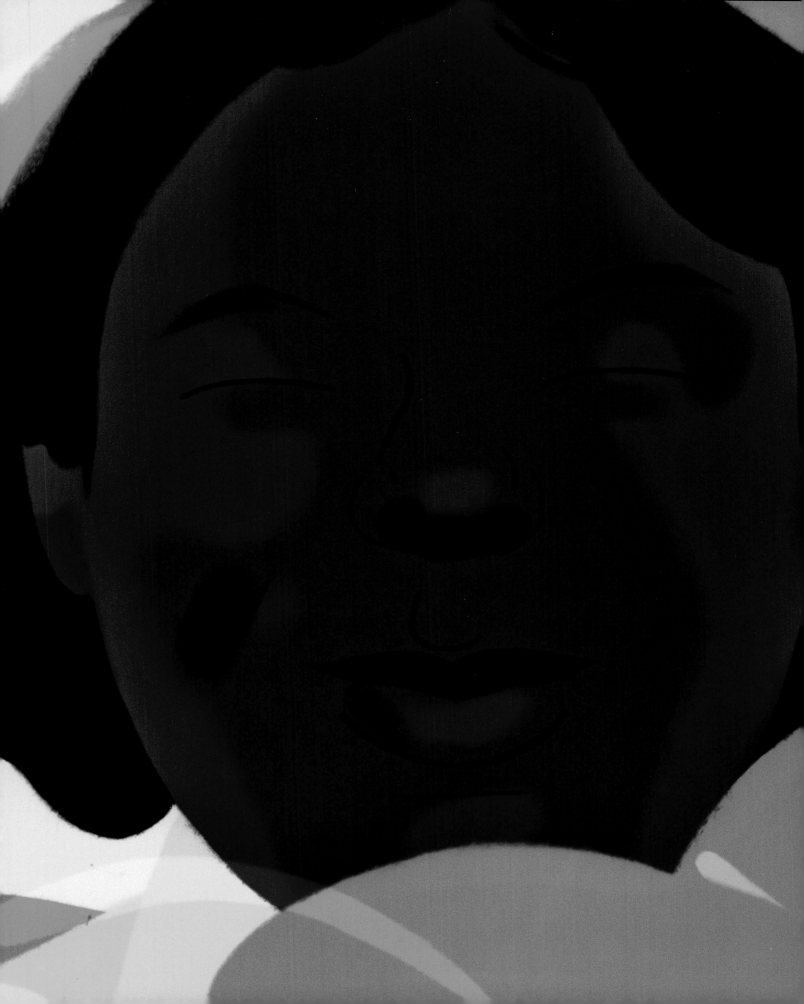

VI

SING a song for Gwendolyn Brooks.
Chicago teems with Black sharecroppers from Dixie towns.

While jobs are scarce in the Great Depression,
Migrants slog and scrounge for decent work.

Gwen is Sweet Sixteen in '33.
She is feathery voice and flickering flame.
She gushes and giggles over Shakespeare sonnets.

Her parents are wise and see her light.
They do not yell, "Go mop the floor!"
And when high school chums must look for work,
Gwendolyn is free to sit and think.

AMBITION

It hurts ~~so much~~ a lot to see the top—
And know you're at the base;
To know some power holds you back
And yet see glory's face!

But all true climbers know that they
Must rise by base degree.
And so they keep on climbing 'til
They find that they are—free!

—1930-1933

She learns to labor for the love of words.
Draft one is shoddy.
Draft two is a thud.

Gwen toils to write one poem each day.
She deletes, rewrites, and starts again.
The simplest verse is a taxing struggle.

Draft three is better.
Draft four is best.
Her couplets waltz with wonderment.

Gwen's confidence is a bud in spring.
Revised . . . revisions make poetry RING!

The *Chicago Defender* welcomes Gwen.
Adults read her rhymes in the poetry section.

Mr. Brooks proclaims to Mrs. Brooks,
"This girl we got is a gifted child."

"And one special day," Mrs. Brooks declares,
"She will be a poet like Paul Dunbar."

VII
SING a song for Gwendolyn Brooks.

CHICAGO!

JAZZ!

BE-BOP!

HEY!

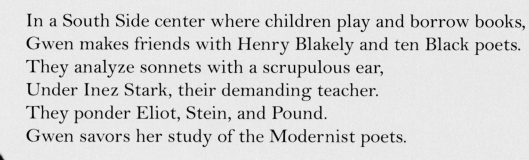

In a South Side center where children play and borrow books,
Gwen makes friends with Henry Blakely and ten Black poets.
They analyze sonnets with a scrupulous ear,
Under Inez Stark, their demanding teacher.
They ponder Eliot, Stein, and Pound.
Gwen savors her study of the Modernist poets.

After scribble, scratch, and sundry rewrites—
Alliterations leap from Gwendolyn's page.

Her words are psalms from a South Side street.
They are polished and poised like English silver.

Gwen enters her poems in magazine contests.
Again and again—she wins first place!

the children of the poor—Sonnet #2

What shall I give my children? who are poor,
Who are adjudged the leastwise of the land,
Who are my sweetest lepers, who demand
No velvet and no velvety velour;
But who have begged me for a brisk contour,
Crying that they are quasi, contraband
Because unfinished, graven by a hand
Less than angelic, admirable or sure.
My hand is stuffed with mode, design, device.
But I lack access to my proper stone.
And plenitude of plan shall not suffice
Nor grief nor love shall be enough alone
To ratify my little halves who bear
Across an autumn freezing everywhere.

—1949

VIII
SING a song for Gwendolyn Brooks.
Time rocks and rolls at a steady pitch.

Gwen graduates college.
Gwen marries Henry.
Gwen "mothers" and "poets" in 1950.

Henry works full time in a shirt and tie.
He earns the "bread" for his wife and son.

And on East 63rd at Champlain,
The family rents two rooms in a kitchenette building.

Gwen's South Side view is an urban suite.
Pointed church steeples pierce the clouds.
Poolroom chaps skip school and smoke.
Four and five families live in one house.

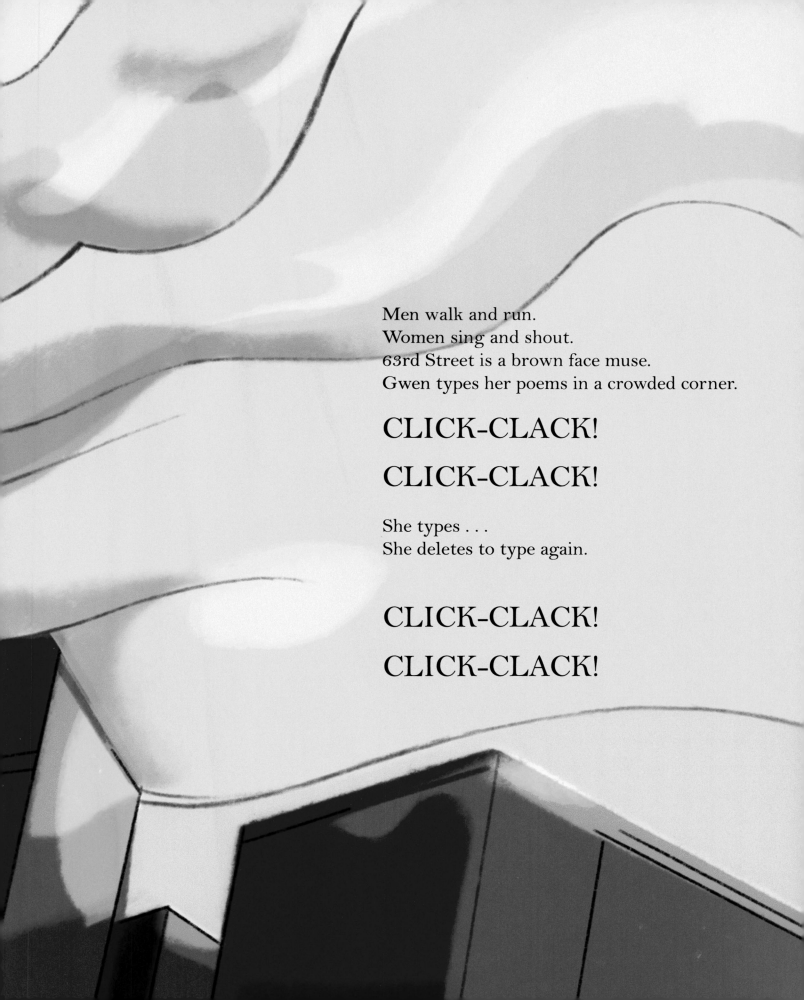

Men walk and run.
Women sing and shout.
63rd Street is a brown face muse.
Gwen types her poems in a crowded corner.

CLICK-CLACK!

CLICK-CLACK!

She types . . .
She deletes to type again.

CLICK-CLACK!

CLICK-CLACK!

Readers crowd bookstores.
They buy Gwen's book and she
Signs her name in a fancy script.

IX
SING a song for Gwendolyn Brooks.
She whittles her sonnets with perfect grace,
Like Edna St. Vincent Millay and Robert Frost.

With slinky, sly, and see-line spunk,
Gwen swings the blues with her black pen,
Like guitar players at Theresa's Lounge.

Gwen paints poems with paintbrush words,
And Gwen takes home a Pulitzer Prize.

A Pulitzer Prize?

A PULITZER PRIZE!

Henry celebrates Gwen.
Junior too.
They shower her with noisy kisses.

Gwendolyn's parents cry tears of joy.
They praise her shine.
They saw it first.

Mr. Brooks and Mrs. Brooks
Planted love and watered it.

Gwendolyn believed.
She found her light.

And—
A furious flower
GREW!

AUTHOR'S NOTE

"No longer walking through rooms, I shall be gone and not gone."
GWENDOLYN BROOKS

GWENDOLYN BROOKS (1917-2000) was an American poet born in Topeka, Kansas. She lived most of her life on the South Side of Chicago, Illinois. Miss Brooks was the first Black writer to win a prestigious Pulitzer Prize. She earned the award in 1950 for her poetry collection *Annie Allen*. These poems are wise, witty, and woeful accounts that capture Black feeling and the urban voice.

Miss Brooks was a ravenous young reader who scribbled rhymes in school notebooks. Her parents, David and Keziah Brooks, nurtured her creativity with free time set aside for writing. When David Brooks saw Gwen engaged in a poem, he released her from doing chores.

Miss Brooks wrote poems to record her ideas about life and the plight of Black people in her Chicago community. So convinced of her daughter's writing future, Keziah Brooks told neighbors often that Gwen would be a famous poet. And in time, Gwendolyn Brooks grew up to write twenty poetry books, two autobiographies, and a novel.

She married Henry Blakely, Jr., in 1939. He wanted to be a writer, too. However, Mr. Blakely sacrificed his ambition to work in the insurance business and care for Gwen and their two children, Henry Blakely III and Nora.

Gwendolyn Brooks was the twenty-ninth poet laureate to the Library of Congress. She was poet laureate for the state of Illinois from 1968 until 2000—the time of her death.

Established writers like Inez Stark, Richard Wright, and Langston Hughes mentored Gwen during the 1940s. Thirty years later, it was Gwendolyn Brooks who shared her knowledge of writing. She mentored Haki Madhubuti and Etheridge Knight—rising young poets from the Black Arts Movement. And in a daring act of love, Miss Brooks invited the Blackstone Rangers Gang to her South Side workshops where she gave lectures on composing sonnets, free verse, and couplets.

From 1950 to this present day, texts by Gwendolyn Brooks have served as required reading in American schools and colleges. She is famous for her mastery of poetic technique, her commitment to racial identity, and her ability to write poems that bridge a gap between formal verse and the common folk. Some of her most popular poems include *Song in the Front Yard, The Bean Eaters, Kitchenette Building*, and *We Real Cool*.

Head wraps and round eyeglasses were hallmarks of Gwendolyn's iconic image. The hallmark of her personality was her generosity. Across five decades, she used portions of her prize money and book advances to sponsor poetry contests for children and adults.

In her lifetime, Gwendolyn Brooks visited Africa and was a noted speaker at American universities. However, Chicago's South Side was her favorite place to live and write. The men, women, and children outside her window inspired her poems. The smells and the sounds from the street put her in a writing mood. Of all these things she said, "That was my material."

Gwendolyn Brooks

TIMELINE

1917: Gwendolyn is born in Topeka, Kansas, on June 7th. The Brooks family makes their permanent home on Chicago's South Side.

1924: She writes her first poem at seven years old.

1925: Gwendolyn's teacher at Forestville School accuses Gwendolyn of plagiarizing a poem. Keziah Brooks brings her daughter to the school. Gwendolyn writes a brilliant poem right in front of the teacher to prove she didn't cheat.*

1933: Her series of apprentice poems are published in the Chicago Defender—a local Black newspaper

1934: Gwendolyn graduates from Englewood High School.

1936: Gwendolyn graduates from Wilson Junior College.

* Though we don't know the teacher's race, only 2.29 percent of Chicago's teaching staff in the era were black, so the artwork shows the teacher here as white, as that was most likely the case.

1939: She marries Henry Lowington Blakely II, and they live on Chicago's South Side.

1940: She gives birth to Henry III.

1941: Gwendolyn, her husband, and a circle of friends study poetry in a writing workshop organized by Inez Stark at the South Side Community Center.

1945: Gwendolyn writes her first poetry book—*A Street in Bronzeville*.

1949: She writes a second poetry book—*Annie Allen*.

1950: Gwendolyn wins a Pulitzer Prize for *Annie Allen*. She is the first Black American to win this award.

1951: She gives birth to her daughter, Nora.

1953: Gwendolyn writes her first and only novel—*Maud Martha*.

1956: She writes a poetry book for children—*Bronzeville Boys and Girls*.

1960: Gwendolyn writes what becomes her most anthologized poem—"We Real Cool" and it is published in her poetry book *The Bean Eaters.*

1967: She visits Fisk University in Nashville for a writers' conference. While there, she meets LeRoi Jones (later known as Amiri Baraka) and pledges her support to the Black Arts Movement.

1968: She writes another poetry book— *In the Mecca.*

1968: Gwendolyn Brooks is named poet laureate of Illinois.

1970: She writes her autobiography—*Report from Part One.*

1985: Gwendolyn is appointed the twenty-ninth poet laureate of the Library of Congress.

1989: She receives the Senior Fellowship in Literature from the National Endowment of the Arts.

1994: Gwendolyn is named Jefferson Lecturer from the National Endowment for the Humanities Lifetime Achievement Award.

1994: She receives the Medal of Distinguished Contributions to American Letters by the National Book Foundation.

1995: She receives the National Medal of Art.

1997: She receives the Lincoln Laureate Award.

2000: Gwendolyn Brooks battles cancer and passes away on December 3, 2000.

SUGGESTED READINGS *by Gwendolyn Brooks*

Brooks, Gwendolyn. *Bronzeville Boys and Girls: Pictures by Faith Ringgold.* New York: Amistad, 2015.

_____. *The Essential Gwendolyn Brooks.* New York: American Poets Project, 2005.

_____. *Selected Poems.* New York: HarperPerennial, 2006.

_____. *The Tiger Who Wore White Gloves.* Chicago: Third World Press, 1974.

BIBLIOGRAPHY

Adoff, Arnold. *The Poetry of Black America; Anthology of the 20th Century.* New York: Harper & Row, 1973.

Brooks, Gwendolyn. *Report from Part One.* Detroit, Michigan: Broadside, 1972.

_____. and Elizabeth Alexander. *The Essential Gwendolyn Brooks.* New York: Library of America, 2005.

_____. and Gloria Jean Wade Gayles. *Conversations with Gwendolyn Brooks.* Jackson: University of Mississippi, 2003.

Kent, George E. *A Life of Gwendolyn Brooks.* Lexington: University Press of Kentucky, 1990.

Mickle, Mildred R. *Critical Insights Gwendolyn Brooks.* Pasadena, Calif.: Salem, 2009.

Wright, Stephen Caldwell. *On Gwendolyn Brooks—Reliant Contemplation.* Ann Arbor: University of Michigan Press, 1996.